SCIENCE MADE SIMPLE™

GASES AND THEIR PROPERTIES

SUSAN MEYER

rosen publishing's
rosen
central®

New York

To Hal Meyer

Published in 2011 by The Rosen Publishing Group, Inc.
29 East 21st Street, New York, NY 10010

First Edition

Library of Congress Cataloging-in-Publication Data

Meyer, Susan, 1986–
Gases and their properties / Susan Meyer. — 1st ed.
   p. cm. — (Science made simple)
Includes bibliographical references and index.
ISBN 978-1-4488-1233-2 (lib. bdg.)
ISBN 978-1-4488-2243-0 (pbk.)
ISBN 978-1-4488-2245-4 (6-pack)
1. Gases—Juvenile literature. 2. Gas laws (Physical chemistry)—
Juvenile literature. I. Title.
QC161.2.M49 2011
530.4'3—dc22

2010015858

Manufactured in Malaysia

CPSIA Compliance Information: Batch #W11YA: For further information, contact Rosen Publishing, New York, New York, at 1-800-237-9932.

On the cover: An artist's rendering of a molecule. In gases, molecules tend to be farther apart from each other and travel faster.

CONTENTS

INTRODUCTION

Matter is all around us. Everything we can touch or breathe is matter. Matter includes everything in existence that takes up space, including things that cannot be seen. On Earth, matter exists in three forms: solid, liquid, and gas. Usually, it is easy to tell the difference between these three states of matter. Clearly, ice is a solid, just as water is a liquid, and steam is a gas. But what exactly is a gas, and what causes it to change from a liquid? Heat causes the molecules in a liquid to move farther apart and become a gas. A gas is a substance whose molecules are very far apart.

Although they can't usually be seen, gases are all around us. And even though these gases are often invisible to the naked eye, people can still feel their effects. The air we breathe is made up of a combination of gases. Gases are made up of molecules, which are groups of atoms. An atom is the smallest unit of an element.

This geothermal energy power plant is releasing one of the most familiar gases: steam. Steam is the gas that results when liquid water is heated to its boiling point.

All matter is made up of atoms. A molecule is one or more atoms joined together. In solids, molecules are close together and they don't move around. In liquids, the molecules are still close together, but they can move around each other. However, the molecules in gases are really far apart. If it were possible for a person to shrink down to the size of a molecule and float around in a gas, he or she would mostly see empty space. The molecules that make up gases are so far apart that about 99 percent of the total volume of gas is just empty space.

The number of elements that appear in their most typical form as a gas are relatively few. They include nitrogen, oxygen, and hydrogen, as well as fluorine and chlorine in the halogen family. There are a handful of others, most notably the noble gases that are grouped together on the periodic table. Yet many substances that ordinarily occur as a solid or a liquid can also appear in the form of a gas. For example, water can take the form of a solid (ice, frost), a liquid, or a gas (steam).

This is true of other gases, such as the gases in air, too. We don't think of nitrogen or oxygen as liquids, however, because they become liquids only at very low temperatures, far below any that we ordinarily experience. At normal temperatures, nitrogen and oxygen can be only gases. We are familiar with liquid water because the temperature at which liquid water cannot exist is much higher than room temperature. Elements that usually appear as solids, such as gold or silver, must be heated to much higher temperatures to convert them completely to gas. In order to create a gas from gold, it would have to be heated to 5,173 degrees Fahrenheit (2,856 degrees Celsius).

Although there are many different kinds of gases in our world, they all have certain things in common that enable scientists to study gases as a group. The qualities shared by all gases are called gas properties. In general, gases respond more dramatically to changes in pressure and temperature than do solids and liquids. This allows scientists to predict gas behaviors more accurately than those of solids and liquids. These predictions can explain everyday occurrences, such as the fact that an open can of soda will soon lose its fizz. But they also apply to more dramatic, life-or-death situations like how a scuba diver can remain alive and breathing, even in very deep water.

THE UNIVERSAL PROPERTIES OF GASES

G as properties can apply to almost any gas. This enables scientists to make general assumptions about how a particular gas will behave under certain conditions. The main properties that scientists have identified are gases' tendency to expand to fit their container, be easily compressed, and be sensitive to changes in pressure and temperature.

EXPANDABILITY

Imagine inflating a balloon versus putting liquid in a cup. The gas used to inflate the balloon is distributed uniformly throughout the balloon. The liquid sits at the bottom of the cup and does not uniformly fill it.

Although gases are often invisible to the naked eye, yellow bromine gas is visible in this photograph. The bromine gas is in the process of expanding to fill its container.

One of the main properties of gases is their expandability. Unlike solids and liquids, gas will expand to fill whatever space is available to it. Also unlike liquids or solids, gases occupy their containers uniformly and completely. The gas's container may be the size of your house, or it may be as small as a closed beaker. It might even be as large as the planet Earth.

One group of gases that everyone is familiar with is found in the compound that forms the air we breathe. This compound is made up of oxygen, nitrogen, argon, carbon dioxide, and other trace gases. You might wonder what keeps the air on Earth from floating off into space. What holds the air is gravity. You may not realize it, but air has weight, just like all other matter on Earth. Gravity holds air like a blanket around the planet. The air is more dense near the surface, where we live, but it gradually becomes less dense at higher levels. It eventually fades away at about 75 miles (120 kilometers) up.

Regardless of the size of its container, a gas will expand to fill it. For this reason, it can usually be assumed that the volume of a gas is equal to the volume of the gas's container. Volume is the amount of space that matter takes up. Gases have no definite volume or shape. They will always conform to the volume and shape of whatever they are contained in.

HEATING AND COOLING

Another important property of gases is how they respond to heat. Why does raising the temperature of a solid cause it to change into a liquid and then into a gas?

All substances are composed of molecules, and all molecules are in motion. The rate of that motion determines how the attraction among the molecules affects them. The force that attracts molecules to molecules is very different from the gravitational force that keeps Earth-bound objects from flying off into space. Instead, the force that attracts molecules to other molecules is electromagnetic.

An electromagnetic force is related to the force that attracts the north pole of one magnet to the south pole of another magnet. Similarly, positive electric charges are attracted to negative electric charges and vice versa. Molecules can have areas of positive charge and other areas of negative charge. The positive area of one molecule attracts the negative area of

The force that attracts the molecules in a gas to one another is similar to the force that attracts the north and south poles of a magnet to each other.

another molecule, and the molecules stick together, like magnets. In a solid or liquid, all of the molecules are stuck together by these electric forces. When a substance is heated, its molecules move faster and faster. Eventually, there comes a point when the molecules are moving so fast they can no longer stick together. When they are moving too fast to stick together, they separate and form a gas. In a gas, the atoms move quickly, are farther apart, and appear to move at random.

Heating a substance can cause it to change from one state of matter to the next. If you heat ice enough, it melts and becomes liquid water. If you heat liquid water to its boiling point, it becomes a gas referred to as steam. These changes are called physical changes because the molecular composition of the substance remains unchanged. The only difference is that because heat was added, the molecules in the substance moved faster and faster. When a solid or liquid turns into a gas, its molecules move farther apart. When a gas is cooled, its molecules will move closer together as long as the volume of the container can change.

This phenomenon can be observed in a simple household experiment. All that is needed are a balloon, some masking tape, and a freezer. Once these materials are assembled, the balloon should be inflated. Blowing into a balloon is actually filling it with a gas—air. The gas expands to fill its container—in this case, the balloon.

Once the balloon is filled and its opening tied off, a piece of masking tape should be wrapped tightly around the fattest part of the balloon. The balloon should then be placed in the freezer overnight. The next day, take the balloon out of the freezer. The tape will have crinkles along its edges. The tape is crinkled because the balloon got smaller while in the freezer. When the temperature of the gas inside the balloon became colder, the gas molecules moved closer together. When the molecules move closer together, the gas takes up less space. For this reason, the volume of the gas gets smaller when the gas is cooled.

After the balloon is taken out of the freezer and left at room temperature, the crinkles on the tape should straighten out. As the gas inside the balloon warms back up, the molecules move apart again, and the balloon stretches back out.

COMPRESSIBILITY

A third primary property of gases is their ability to be compressed, also called their compressibility. Gases are much easier to compress than solids or liquids. Compressing matter means applying pressure to it to make it smaller. If you push down on a solid, like a wooden or metal table, you will find that your actions don't have much of an effect. The table will not change its shape in any way. This is because solids are not easily compressed, since their molecules are close together and do not have a lot of space between them. Liquids are also not easily compressed, though they are slightly more compressible than solids because their molecules are spaced a little farther apart.

Gases, on the other hand, can be easily compressed. Because the molecules of a gas are so far apart, it means they have a lot more empty space between them. When a force is applied to a gas, the molecules easily move closer together, absorbing the force. If the gas molecules hadn't started so far apart with

Fast Gas

The molecules in oxygen gas travel at an average speed of 1,056 miles per hour (1,700 kilometers per hour) on a warm day. That's faster than a jet airplane! However, inside a room, the oxygen molecules can't move very far. This is because they crash into other oxygen gas molecules on a frequent basis. Each molecule has about four or five billion collisions with other molecules every second.

This isn't just true of oxygen molecules. Most gas molecules travel fast enough that if they were the only molecule in the room, they could cross it almost instantly. However, when a gas with a strong odor is released in one corner of a room, it can take several minutes for the smell of the gas to reach the other end of the room. Because of the billions of collisions that gas molecules endure within an enclosed space such as a room, their path is filled with detours, which greatly increase the time it takes to cross the room.

so much space between them, they wouldn't have had enough room to be compressed closer together.

PRESSURE

Heating causes molecules in a gas to move farther apart. Heating also causes them to increase in speed. Molecules in a cooler gas will move at slower speeds than molecules in a warmer gas. Although gas molecules are relatively far apart in a gas, they still often crash into each other because they move at such high speeds. These collisions are what cause gas pressure. Gas pressure is produced by the force of all the molecules colliding against each other and against the sides of their container. When there are fewer molecules bouncing around hitting each other and the container, the pressure is lower. When there are more molecules hitting each other and the sides of the container, the pressure increases.

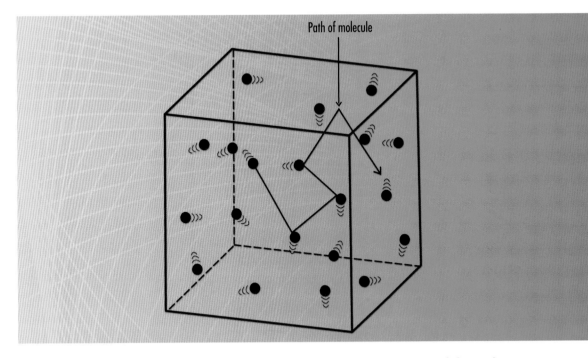

Path of molecule

Gases are comprised of many constantly moving molecules. The more compressed the gas is, the higher the gas pressure and the more rapid the movement of the molecules.

The pressure a gas exerts on its environment is one of its essential properties. The pressure of the gas becomes greater as more gas is added to a container. The more gas added to a container, the greater the concentration of gas molecules. The more gas molecules present in a container, the closer together they will be and the more collisions there will be among molecules and between molecules and the sides of their container.

This crowding and the resulting collisions increase the gas pressure. Think of it as a bumper car ride at a fair. The more people driving bumper cars, the less space there will be, the harder it will be to move around, and the more likely it will be that crashes will occur between cars and between cars and the walls.

The force that causes a kernel of popcorn to burst into a delicious snack food is caused by a buildup of high gas pressure within the kernel.

Another everyday example of the pressure produced by gas can be observed during the making of popcorn. When kernels of popcorn are heated, the liquids within the kernel are turned to gases by the increasing heat. In the enclosed space of the kernel, the molecules heat up, begin moving faster and faster, and collide into each other and with the shell of the kernel many times. This causes gas pressure to build up inside the kernel. The pressure becomes so enormous that is causes the kernel to explode, releasing the pent-up and pressurized gas. The result is popcorn!

2

THE GAS LAWS

G ases have certain uniform properties that can be observed when studying them. Because many properties of gases do not depend on the identity of the gas, it is possible for scientists to make general assumptions about the characteristics and behavior of gases as a group. Yet there are several variables to consider when studying gases. These include the volume of the gas, its temperature, the number of molecules in the gas, and the pressure exerted on the gas.

Many chemists have studied gases over the years and, using the universal properties common to all gases, have discovered laws that can be applied to almost any particular gas. These laws describe the relationships between volume, pressure, temperature, and the number of molecules in the gas. Collectively, these laws are known as the gas laws. The most important include Boyle's law, Charles's law, Avogadro's law, and Dalton's law. They are all named for the scientists whose work led to their discovery. There is also the ideal gas law, which combines the other laws.

BOYLE'S LAW

Because air is a compound of several different gases, humans are used to living with a certain amount of gas pressure called air pressure. In fact, people are so used to air pressure that they seldom notice it (though some people get strong headaches or other body aches if the air pressure changes dramatically in a short period of time, such as before major storms). Humans normally don't feel the air pressure that is exerted on them because the human body is primarily made up of liquid. As mentioned in chapter 1, liquids aren't very compressible. Thus, the human body is not greatly affected by increases or decreases in air pressure.

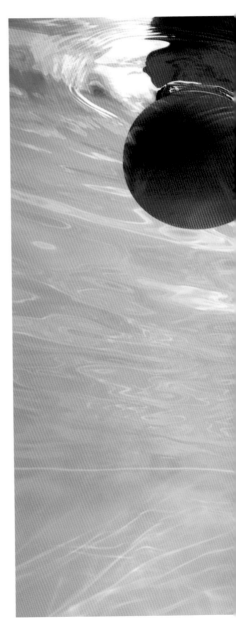

If one of these balloons is pushed farther under the surface of the water, the additional pressure of the water will exert higher pressure on the gas inside the balloon. This will cause the gas to compress and the balloon to get smaller.

There are times when people do notice changes in pressure, primarily in their ears. Our ears "pop" when we're on airplanes or driving on high mountain roads because they have pockets of air in them. And that air, like all gases, is compressible. When

people reach high altitudes, there are fewer gas molecules in the air, so the outside air pressure is less. The pressure within the air pockets of the ear, however, remains higher than the outside air pressure. This difference in the two air pressures causes the air in the ears to expand, resulting in a popping feeling as the air escapes.

A gas will compress proportionately to the amount of pressure exerted on it. For example, take a balloon that measures 1 cubic foot (0.03 cubic meters) in volume and double the pressure on it. The balloon will be compressed to ½ cubic foot (0.01 m³). Increase the amount of pressure on the balloon by four times and the balloon will be compressed to ¼ cubic foot (0.0071 m³). This theory is known as Boyle's law. Boyle's law states that the volume of gas is inversely proportional to the pressure exerted on it.

Another example can also be shown with the help of a balloon. A balloon with a volume of 1 cubic foot (0.03 m³) floats on the surface of a pool of water. The only pressure currently being exerted on the balloon is the amount of air pressure that is constantly present at sea level. Pressure is measured in standard atmospheres (atm). At sea level, the air pressure is known to be about 1 atm. If the balloon is pushed under the water to a depth at which it is now under 2 atm of pressure (1 atm from the air above it and 1 atm from the water above it), the amount of pressure on the balloon will have doubled.

Boyle's law states that since twice the original amount of pressure is now acting on the balloon, the volume of the balloon should have decreased by one half, to ½ cubic feet (0.01 m³). If the balloon is submerged deeper and deeper in the water, the pressure exerted on it will continue to increase as its volume continues to decrease. If 3 atm of pressure are placed on the submerged balloon (three times the amount of pressure originally exerted on it), it should be reduced to one-third of its original volume (0.33 ft³; 0.0093 m³). Similarly, if 6 atm of pressure are placed on the balloon, the balloon should be reduced to one-sixth of its original volume (0.17 ft³; 0.0048 m³).

If the balloon is brought back to the surface of the water, the pressure exerted on it will return to 1 atm, and it should return

Gas Laws and the Bends

Gas laws aren't just ideas that work on paper. They also provide lifesaving knowledge for people such as scuba divers. Imagine what would happen if a gas were to bubble out of one's blood like carbon dioxide bubbling out of a can of soda. This is exactly what can happen to an undersea diver who returns to the surface too quickly.

Nitrogen, a gas found in air, dissolves in the blood when placed under the higher pressure of deep water. If a diver returns too quickly to the surface and the change to lower pressure is too abrupt, the dissolving nitrogen can create bubbles that block oxygen absorption and can be quite painful. This produces decompression sickness, also known as the bends. The condition can result in impaired judgment, confusion, poor concentration, an inability to perform basic or routine tasks, hallucinations, and blackouts. If a scuba diver is not careful, he or she can die from the bends.

The deeper a gas is underwater, the greater the amount of pressure. When nitrogen in the air tank becomes pressurized and is breathed in by the diver, it will enter the bloodstream but soon dissolve into bubbles, creating the narcotic effect of the bends.

To avoid this, scuba divers breathe a mix of oxygen and helium in their tanks. Unlike nitrogen, helium gas does not dissolve so easily in the blood, and thus it is safer for a diver to inhale this oxygen-helium mixture. Divers also ascend slowly to the surface, taking breaks along the way, to allow the water pressure being exerted on their bodies to decrease gradually.

to its original volume (1 ft³; 0.03 m³). The air in the balloon was compressed due to the added pressure acting on it by the water when it was submerged. Once it is no longer submerged and returns to the normal air pressure above the surface of the water, the gas within it should return to its original volume.

CHARLES'S LAW

Have you ever wondered how a hot-air balloon is able to lift a heavy basket and several people weighing hundreds of pounds each high up into the air? The answer can be found in another one of the gas laws, Charles's law. This law states that the volume of an amount of gas increases or decreases by the same amount as its temperature increases or decreases.

The reason a hot-air balloon is able to float so high and bear so much weight is that the air inside it is not as dense as the air outside it. According to Charles's law, when the air in a balloon is heated, its volume will increase,

The heated air inside a hot-air balloon is lighter than the cooler air outside it. This gives the hot-air balloon the buoyancy it needs to become a high-flying vehicle.

causing the balloon to expand. The relationship between the temperature of a gas and its volume is directly related. If the absolute temperature of a gas is doubled, the volume of that gas will also double. If the absolute temperature of a

gas is tripled, its volume will also triple. The increased volume of the air allows the balloon to fill, and its higher temperature makes it lighter than the colder air outside the balloon (hot air has less mass than colder air). The result is buoyancy within the balloon that allows it to lift off the ground and bear weight.

AVOGADRO'S LAW

From Boyle's law, it is known that the pressure exerted on a gas is inversely proportional to the gas's volume. This means the more pressure exerted on a gas, the smaller its volume will be (the less space it will occupy). And from Charles's law, it is known that the temperature of a gas and its volume are directly related. This means the higher the temperature of a gas, the greater its volume (the more space it will occupy).

However, there is a third important gas law that deals with the volume of a gas. Avogadro's law states that equal volumes of gases that are at the same temperature and pressure contain the same number of molecules, regardless of their distinct chemical nature and physical properties.

Let's say we had two equally sized containers and filled each of them with a gas, one with oxygen and the other with helium. Because of the universal properties of gases, we know that the gases will expand to completely fill their containers. Thus, since the containers are of equal size, the volume of the two gases will also be the same. Now, if we subject both containers of gases to the same temperature and pressure, the containers of oxygen and helium would contain the same number of molecules, according to Avogadro's law. This is true even though oxygen is many times heavier and denser than helium. As long as the pressure, volume, and temperature of the two different gases remain identical, the number of molecules in each would be equal.

DALTON'S LAW

When scientists want to collect a sample of gas, they often do so by using water. The scientists fill a container with water before adding a gas to displace the water. This way, they know the container is full of the gas when all water has been displaced from the container. They do this because gases usually can't be seen, so it can be hard to know when the container has been completely filled with a gas. A problem with this method is that because the gas will have mixed with water, it will likely no longer be pure. Water in the form of gas—water vapor— will now be mixed with the gas as the result of the two coming into contact with each other. To deal with this problem, scientists can use another of the gas laws, Dalton's law.

Dalton's law, sometimes known as the law of partial pressures, states that the total pressure in a container of gas is the sum of the partial pressures of all the gases in the container. Let's say there is a container that has two gases in it: oxygen gas and nitrogen gas. The total pressure of the gas in the container will equal the pressure produced by the oxygen, plus the pressure produced by the nitrogen.

So when scientists want to figure out the pressure produced by a gas that is mixed with water vapor, using Dalton's law, all they have to do is subtract the pressure produced by the

This scientist is using a gas chromatograph machine. The machine is used to separate different gases in a compound so that they can be studied. Using the law of partial pressures, the scientist can determine the pressure caused by each gas in a compound.

water vapor. The remaining pressure will be the pressure of the gas they are studying.

IDEAL GAS LAW

Boyle's law states that the volume of a gas is linked to the amount of pressure exerted on it. Charles's law states that the temperature of a gas and its volume are also linked. From Avogadro's law, it is known that if the volume, temperature, and pressure of two or more gases are constant (whether it's the same kind of gas or different gases), the number of gas molecules in each container will be the same. All of these theories apply equally to any gas and work with the same concepts: pressure, volume, temperature, and the number of molecules in a gas. For these reasons, it was only a matter of time before scientists combined them into a single, more general law called the ideal gas law.

The ideal gas law states that the pressure produced by the gas multiplied by the volume of the gas is equal to the number of molecules in the gas multiplied by the temperature of the gas and by a gas constant. It is easier to visualize the concept with this equation:

$$pV=nRT$$

In this equation, p is equal to the pressure of the gas. V is the volume of the gas. N is the number of molecules in the gas. R is a gas constant. T is the temperature. The gas constant R is a physical constant that is used in a number of equations in the physical sciences. It was discovered when scientists realized that if they knew a gas's pressure, volume, and number of molecules and plugged these values into the equation above, that the result for R was always the same.

The ideal gas law makes studying gases much easier. Because of it, one only needs to know three out of four of the variables in order to solve for the fourth variable. If the pressure, volume, and temperature of the gas are known, the equation makes it easy to determine how many molecules are in the gas. If the temperature, number of molecules, and volume of the gas are known, the pressure produced by the gas will also be easy to determine.

3

THE SCIENTISTS BEHIND THE GAS LAWS

Most of the gas laws mentioned in chapter 2 were named for the people who discovered them. While scientists now consider these laws a standard and accepted part of studying gases, they were once considered revolutionary. The men who discovered these gas laws all used precise experiments and careful thinking to reach conclusions that continue to inform our modern understanding of gases, their properties, and their behaviors.

ROBERT BOYLE

Robert Boyle (1627–1691) was a seventeenth-century chemist from Ireland who came up with the idea that the pressure exerted on a gas and its

Robert Boyle was a seventeenth-century chemist who did much to advance the study of pressure on gases. His studies led to the discovery of a gas law that bears his name.

volume is inversely proportional. But how did Boyle discover the law that now bears his name?

In 1662, he created a tool for measuring pressure so that he could study the relationship between pressure and the volume of gases. He took a piece of glass tubing that was shaped like a J and sealed it on the shorter end. He then trapped some gas in the sealed end of the tube by pouring varying amounts of mercury into the open end. The different amounts of mercury varied the pressure on the trapped gas. Each time Boyle changed the pressure, he measured the volume of the gas in the end of the tube. His experiment was done using a fixed amount of gas that was at a constant temperature. In this way, Boyle was able to ensure that changes in the quantity or temperature of the gas would not be part of what affected changes in volume. Only changes in pressure would be responsible for any changes in the gas's volume.

JACQUES CHARLES

Jacques Charles (1746–1823) was a chemist, physicist, and balloon enthusiast born in Loiret, France. Hot-air balloons were extremely popular in eighteenth-century France. Charles's significant contribution to the study of gases came as a result of his interest in improving the performance of hot-air balloons. He wanted to better understand the relationship between temperature and volume for a gas.

When Robert Boyle performed his experiments in the seventeenth century, he made sure to keep all factors constant except for pressure and volume. Jacques Charles did something similar

French scientist Jacques Charles was the first man to use hydrogen gas in hot-air balloons.

with his experiment. He kept all factors constant except for temperature and volume. The equipment used by Charles was also similar to that used in Boyle's experiment more than one hundred years earlier. Just like Boyle, Charles trapped a quantity of gas in a J-shaped glass tube that was sealed at one end. Next, Charles placed this tube in a water bath. By changing the temperature of the water, he was able to change the temperature of the gas. Charles, like Boyle, used mercury in his experiment.

However, unlike Boyle, Charles used mercury to make sure that the pressure stayed constant instead of using it to add pressure to the gas. By adjusting the mercury to balance it, Charles could make sure that the pressure exerted on the gas stayed at 1 atm (normal air pressure), even when it was submerged in water. This way, pressure was not a factor in how the gas's volume changed. Charles's experiment could focus only on how temperature changes affected the volume of the gas.

Absolute Zero

What Jacques Charles learned in his experiment was that if he increased the temperature of the gas, he could also increase its volume. Conversely, he discovered that if he decreased the gas's temperature, he could decrease its volume. But if a decrease in gas temperature results in a decrease in its volume, what happens if the temperature is lowered to a point at which the gas's volume drops to zero? It is impossible to have a negative volume, so the temperature at which the volume drops to zero must, in some sense, be the lowest temperature that can be achieved. This temperature is called absolute zero.

Charles determined that the temperature at which gases cease to have any volume is -459.67°F (or -273.15°C). At absolute zero, molecules have the smallest amount of energy possible and have almost entirely ceased moving back and forth.

JOHN DALTON

John Dalton (1766–1844) was an English chemist, meteorologist, and physicist. Many historians think that Dalton chose to study gases and pressure because of his interest in meteorology, which is the study of weather. When he was a young man, Dalton joined the Manchester Literary and Philosophical Society. Soon after joining, he published his first book, *Meteorological Observations and Essays*. In this book, Dalton presented, for the first time, his ideas on gases. Specifically, he discussed his finding that, in a mixture of gases, each gas exists independently of the others and acts accordingly.

Once he started to study gases, Dalton was able to perform a series of experiments. This led him to the law of partial pressures, which now bears his name. Dalton demonstrated that if two gases are mixed together, they behave as if they are totally

The English chemist John Dalton published many works on gases and chemistry in general. This chart shows some of Dalton's work on the table of elements.

independent of each other. The first gas does not attract or repel the second gas; instead it seems to "ignore" it entirely. The result is that the total pressure exerted by the mixture of gases is the sum of the separate pressures exerted by each separate gas in the mixture or compound. Although, Dalton later discovered that gases don't always "ignore" each other entirely, his law of partial pressures is still very useful to scientists to this day.

AMEDEO AVOGADRO

Amedeo Avogadro (1776–1856) was a physicist, chemist, and mathematician born in Turin, Italy. Using the work of Dalton, Charles, and Boyle, Avogadro went one step further with his work. He suggested that equal volumes of all gases at the same temperature and pressure contain the same number of molecules. This is now known as Avogadro's law.

THE ROLE OF GASES IN EVERYDAY LIFE

Most of the breakthroughs in the study of gases and their properties discussed in the previous chapter occurred more than one hundred years ago. However, much work has been done in the study of gases since then. Scientists have used what they know about gases to invent many products that have made life for people easier, safer, more comfortable, and more convenient. These include products to improve people's safety like the air bag or the fire extinguisher, new forms of energy known as gas hydrates that can make our energy use more productive, and even products that are merely pleasurable, such as a can of carbonated soda.

FIRE EXTINGUISHERS

Having a fire extinguisher in the house is an essential part of fire safety. If a fire breaks out, it needs to be put out quickly before it spreads to other areas and becomes too large and hot to fight effectively. Often, by the time the fire department arrives on the scene, gets set up, and begins turning the hoses on, it is too late to save the house. But how exactly does a fire extinguisher work? And why is it better than just pouring buckets of water on a fire?

A common type of fire extinguisher consists of a metal cylinder with an operating lever at the top. Inside the cylinder is a tube of compressed carbon dioxide surrounded by a quantity of water, which creates pressure around the carbon dioxide tube. When the operating lever is depressed, it activates a spring mechanism. This mechanism opens the release valve at the top of the tube of carbon dioxide. When the valve opens, the carbon dioxide escapes into the extra space created by the air pocket, exerting high pressure on the water.

This high-pressure mixture of water and carbon dioxide goes rushing out of the tube, which was opened when the release lever was pressed. All of this happens in a fraction of a second, giving a person plenty of time to put out a small fire that has just started.

Carbon dioxide is used in fire extinguishers because it helps smother the fire by depriving it of oxygen. At the same time, the water cools what is burning. A fire needs oxygen and heat to keep it burning. If the fire's source of oxygen is removed, it will go out. If the fire is cooled, it will go out even faster. This

Many people know fire extinguishers can save the day in the event of a fire. But not everyone knows that what makes fire extinguishers work is pressurized carbon dioxide gas that is stored inside the vessel.

is why throwing blankets, dirt, or sand on top of small fires can also smother flames.

AIR BAGS

Most cars these days come equipped with air bags in the driver's and front passenger's seats. In fact, since 1998, new cars in the United States are legally required to have air bags. Some cars also come with optional side-collision air bags that can also be placed in rear passenger seats. The idea behind air bags is to have a large pillow inflate when the car is involved in a crash. This pillow keeps drivers and passengers from hitting the hard surfaces of the car such as the dashboard or, worse yet, the windshield.

The design of the air bag includes a sensor that determines in a split second if the car has hit something. When the sensor detects that the car has hit something with force, it triggers the immediate release of two gases that react to create a small explosion that produces nitrogen gas. This nitrogen gas fills the bag instantaneously, causing it to inflate.

The extreme pressure caused by the nitrogen gas suddenly filling the bag causes the bag to burst out of the compartment where it is normally stored. The bag bursts from its storage site at about 200 miles per hour (322 km/h). The entire process of air bag inflation only takes about one-twenty-fifth of a second, faster than the blink of an eye. It is very important that the bag fills with gas quickly and the pressure of the gas is high enough for the bag to burst out of its compartment. The speed at which an air bag inflates is crucial to its ability to prevent serious injuries in the event of a car crash. An air bag that is

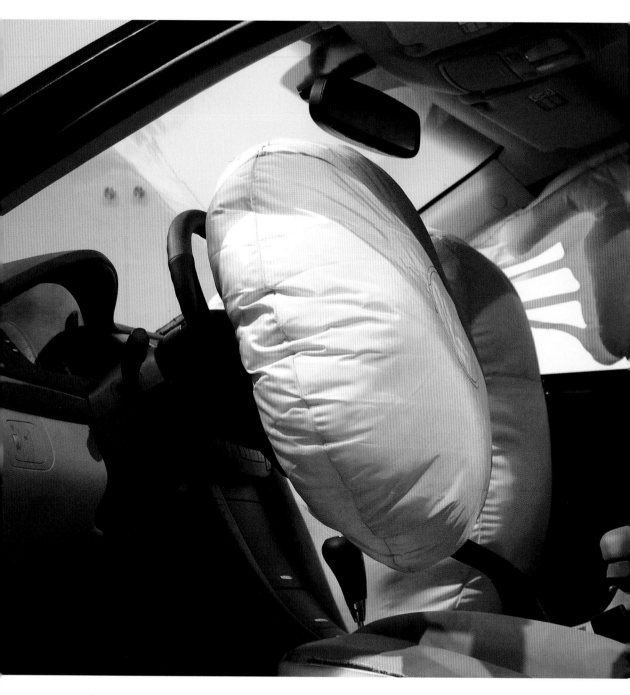

An air bag can save lives by rapidly filling with air in the event of a car crash. The air bag is able to inflate in a fraction of a second because it is filled with nitrogen gas kept under pressure.

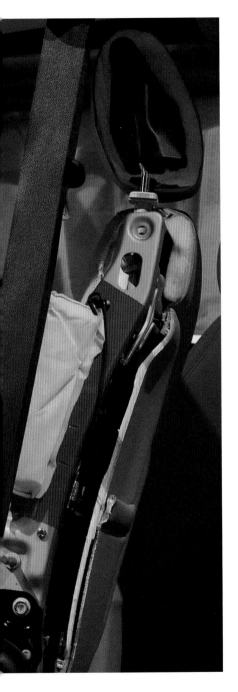

only partially inflated at the moment of impact will not protect the driver or passenger from injury.

CARBONATED SODA

No matter what the flavor of soda, whether clear, cola, or fruity, what makes it soda are the bubbles. Every can of soda is bubbly because it contains carbon dioxide (this is why we call them carbonated drinks). Have you ever noticed that no bubbles can be seen in an unopened bottle of soda? This is because when the soda is packaged at the factory, the carbon dioxide gas is dissolved into the liquid, put in bottles (or cans), and sealed under high pressure. When this happens, the water molecules surround the gas molecules of carbon dioxide and keep them from coming together to form bubbles of gas.

When a bottle of soda is opened, bubbles form. This is because, once the bottle is opened, the carbon dioxide gas is no longer pressurized. Without pressure being exerted on it, the gas expands. The gas molecules of carbon dioxide are then able to come together to make bubbles.

A refreshing glass of soda just wouldn't be soda without the carbonation. The little bubbles form in soda when the can or bottle is opened and the pressurized carbon dioxide is released.

Why does shaking a can make the carbonated soda spurt out in a fizzy spray? The can contains a small amount of carbon dioxide gas under pressure. Usually, this is at the top of the can. When the can is opened, the gas escapes. When an unopened can is shaken, some of the carbon dioxide gas forms bubbles that stick to the inside surface of the can, below the surface of the liquid. When the shaken can is opened, these bubbles rapidly expand, pushing the liquid up and out of the can.

The reaction is similar to what happens when an air bag inflates. However, the gas pressure of a carbonated drink is much less strong. The gas pressure in a can of soda is not nearly enough to burst through the can, as an air bag can and must burst through its storage container.

Mint Fizz

Have you ever seen someone drop Mentos mint candies into a 2-liter (0.5 gallon) bottle of soda? The result is a geyser of cola spilling out of the bottle. This happens for much the same reason that shaking a bottle of soda causes it to whoosh out of the bottle. Remember that the carbon dioxide molecules in the soda are surrounded by water molecules that trap them and prevent bubble formation. Once the water molecules separate from the carbon dioxide molecules, however, bubbles start to form—and they can form very quickly.

The trick is separating the carbon dioxide from the water molecules so that they can begin to form bubbles. The surface of an object provides a place for carbon dioxide molecules to cling together to begin forming bubbles. Once a few molecules come together, others will quickly follow. The surface of a Mentos candy is fairly coarse and uneven. Because it has so many little nooks and crannies, a Mentos candy provides a lot of places for carbon dioxide molecules to grasp onto. This allows a lot of bubbles to form. When this happens, the bubbles burst up out of the soda bottle creating a geyser of fizzy liquid.

METHANE HYDRATES

Methane is a colorless, odorless gas that is frequently found in nature. It is the principal component of natural gas. The abundance of methane gas on Earth makes it a good source for fuel. Sometimes methane gas gets trapped by water molecules. This is very similar to what occurs at soda bottling factories during the carbonation process.

If the conditions are right and a large amount of pressure exists in cold temperatures, the methane gas molecules can be trapped inside pieces of ice. These are called methane hydrates. Methane hydrates can form deep in the ocean or in very cold places like the Arctic under blocks of ice. In illustrating Boyle's law, we observed how pushing a balloon deeper and deeper underwater increased the pressure on the gas. The pressure is even more immense on the ocean floor because of all the water lying on top of it. It is also usually very cold

This photograph shows some of the methane hydrates found in the Blake Ridge, located in the Atlantic Ocean, off the coast of South Carolina.

on the ocean floor. These cold, high-pressure conditions are perfect for the formation of methane hydrates.

Scientists have recently started looking at methane hydrates as a possible source of fuel. We know from Boyle's law that

when the pressure increases, the volume of a gas decreases. Because of the extreme pressure pushing down on it, the methane gas trapped inside methane hydrates is super concentrated, occupying very little space. This highly pressurized gas has the potential to be an excellent and highly efficient energy source. A tiny chunk of methane hydrate could provide a lot of energy to fuel cars, heat homes, or power factories because the gas is so concentrated—so much energy is contained within a very small package. Because of its potential as an energy source, methane hydrates are sometimes called "ice that burns."

Scientists are currently looking for ways to harvest methane so that it could potentially be used to meet future energy needs. This research is especially important because current fossil fuel energy sources are believed to be contributing to very serious environmental problems associated with pollution, global warming, and climate change.

5

GREENHOUSE GASES AND GLOBAL WARMING

Earth's atmosphere is composed of gases. Almost 80 percent of our atmosphere is made up of nitrogen, and most of the rest is oxygen. The remainder of the atmosphere is composed of small percentages of argon, carbon dioxide, neon, helium, and water vapor. Earth's atmosphere is all around us. It is the air we breathe.

THE GREENHOUSE EFFECT IN THE ATMOSPHERE

In recent years, we have heard a lot about greenhouse gases in the atmosphere and some of the problems that they are causing for Earth and all of the planet's life-forms. Why are these potentially harmful gases referred to as greenhouse gases?

Greenhouse gases in the atmosphere behave much like the glass panes in a greenhouse. One of the properties of greenhouse gases is their ability to absorb heat and keep it from escaping. Sunlight enters Earth's atmosphere, passing through the blanket of gases. As the rays reach Earth's surface, the planet's land and bodies of water absorb the sunlight's energy. Once absorbed, this energy is sent back into the atmosphere as heat. Some of the energy passes back into space, but much of it remains trapped in the atmosphere by greenhouse gases, causing the world below to heat up.

The atmosphere is very important for this reason. If we didn't have an atmosphere composed of heat-trapping gases,

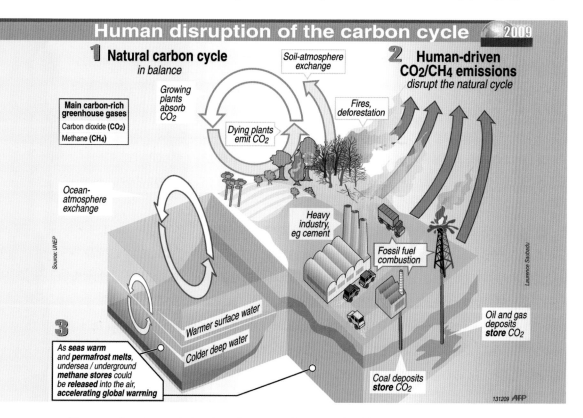

Human disruption of the carbon cycle · 2009

1 Natural carbon cycle *in balance*

Soil-atmosphere exchange

2 Human-driven CO₂/CH₄ emissions *disrupt the natural cycle*

Main carbon-rich greenhouse gases
Carbon dioxide (CO₂)
Methane (CH₄)

Growing plants absorb CO₂

Fires, deforestation

Dying plants emit CO₂

Ocean-atmosphere exchange

Heavy industry, eg cement

Fossil fuel combustion

Warmer surface water

Colder deep water

Oil and gas deposits store CO₂

3 As **seas warm** and **permafrost melts**, undersea / underground **methane stores** could be **released** into the air, **accelerating global warming**

Coal deposits store CO₂

Source: UNEP

Laurence Saubadu

131209 AFP

The normal carbon cycle has been interrupted as a result of factories and machines that generate carbon emissions. These human-made creations produce greater quantities of carbon dioxide gas, which are released into the atmosphere and trap more heat close to Earth's surface.

our planet would be unbearably hot during the day and frigid at night. In this way, the atmospheric gases act like insulation, ensuring that too much radiation from the sun doesn't reach our atmosphere and scorch the planet and too much heat from the planet's surface doesn't leak out into space, leaving Earth frozen.

GREENHOUSE GASES AND HUMANITY'S CARBON FOOTPRINT

While greenhouse gases are an important part of Earth's ability to support life, there is such a thing as too much of a good thing. The amount of greenhouse gases in our atmosphere is currently increasing, due primarily to the burning of fossil fuels. As this happens, more heat is trapped by the gases and is unable to escape back into space. This extra heat continues to radiate around our Earth and gets absorbed by our oceans.

The added heat causes the oceans on our planet to warm. This, in turn, has a number of negative effects on the environment. Warmer oceans cause changes in the ocean currents, which can affect weather patterns. Changes in ocean temperatures also cause polar ice caps to melt, which can cause the water level of the oceans to rise, potentially swamping or flooding small islands and lowland coastal areas. Warmer oceans also increase the amount of water vapor in the air, which can lead to heavier rains and snow in some regions.

What causes the greenhouse gases in the atmosphere to build up? One of the main problems is that too many gases are being released as a result of human activities. The most important of these is carbon dioxide.

Deforestation is one cause of increasing carbon dioxide levels in the atmosphere. Trees absorb carbon dioxide and keep it from building up in the atmosphere. When forests are cut down, it means less carbon dioxide will be absorbed and more will build up in the atmosphere.

There has been much discussion lately of our individual and collective carbon footprint. One's carbon footprint is how much carbon dioxide a person releases into the atmosphere through his or her everyday activities. Burning fossil fuels like coal and oil cause carbon dioxide and other heat-trapping greenhouse gases to be released into the air. Most of the energy that we use to heat our homes and offices and power our cars, computers, appliances, and industrial machines comes from these fossil fuels. Whenever you turn on a light in your home or drive a car, you are producing carbon emissions that are released into the atmosphere (unless your home is powered by alternative energies, such as wind or solar energy, or your car is electric).

Another problem that is causing more greenhouse gases to accumulate in the atmosphere is deforestation—the cutting down of trees. Trees and other plants absorb carbon dioxide in order to grow. When we cut down a large number of trees, there are fewer to absorb all the extra carbon dioxide being produced by our industries, homes, offices, cars, and other machines. The deforestation of many areas of the planet contributes to the problem of greenhouse gases building up in the atmosphere, where still more heat is trapped. This results in higher global surface temperatures and climate change.

REDUCING OUR CARBON FOOTPRINT

There are simple, everyday actions that we can take to lower our own carbon footprint. We can walk, ride bicycles, or take public transportation—such as buses or trains—instead of always traveling by car. We can avoid wasting electricity by turning off lights and unplugging electronics like televisions and computers when they are not in use. More energy-efficient products can be purchased, such as compact fluorescent lightbulbs. These lightbulbs provide the same wattage but use much less energy and last many times longer than regular incandescent lightbulbs.

Reducing, reusing, and recycling waste can also lessen the amount of garbage that ends up in landfills and ultimately pollutes our soil and waterways. Packaging like soda cans requires a lot of energy and materials to create. So anything that can be recycled should be so that those materials can be reused and to reduce the consumption of Earth's dwindling and nonrenewable natural resources.

Joining local tree planting and reforestation projects will also help reduce a locality's carbon footprint by helping foster carbon-consuming vegetation. In addition to these simple lifestyle changes and green activities, we can also encourage friends, family members, neighbors, classmates, town governments, and fellow citizens to reduce their individual carbon footprints and that of the entire community.

A Global Problem Requires Global Solutions

Many countries around the world are concerned about the consequences of producing too many greenhouse gases. In 1997, several countries met to sign an agreement in Kyoto, Japan. The Kyoto Protocol is an agreement among the nations who signed it to reduce the amount of greenhouse gases that their countries produce. These nations agreed to reduce greenhouse gases to a percentage of the levels produced in 1990 by the year 2012. Each country involved in the Kyoto Protocol has a different target based on how industrialized it is and how much it can afford to reduce its industrial output. The United States, under President George W. Bush, refused to sign the agreement.

In December 2009, the world's nations met again in Copenhagen, Denmark, for a climate summit. The end result was an agreement among more than 110 nations—including the largest greenhouse gas emitters such as the United States, Russia, China, India, Japan, and the European Union—to limit global warming to below 3.6°F (2°C) above preindustrial average global temperatures, largely through emissions reduction.

THE PROMISE AND PERIL OF GASES

The general laws and unique properties of gases are important to understand. Gases, such as the greenhouse gases in our atmosphere, can both nurture life on Earth and destabilize or even threaten it. Understanding gases and how they behave can help explain how a kernel of popcorn pops or why a hot-air balloon is able to fly high above the ground. Gases are all around us every day. Understanding the properties of gases is an important part of understanding how the world around us works and how we can ensure that it continues to work and sustain life.

GLOSSARY

absolute zero The lowest possible temperature; -459.67°F (-273.15°C).

atom The smallest unit of matter.

boiling point The temperature at which a liquid turns into a gas. The boiling point of substances can vary a great deal depending on their chemical composition.

carbon emissions Carbon dioxide that is released into the atmosphere, primarily through the burning of fossil fuels.

carbon footprint The amount of carbon dioxide a person releases into the atmosphere through daily activities like driving a car, using electricity, and heating the home with oil.

compressibility The ability to occupy less space. Gases have a high level of compressibility.

constant A number that doesn't change.

electromagnetic force The force that binds atoms to atoms or molecules to molecules.

gas pressure The force created by the molecules in a gas as they collide against their container.

gas properties The characteristics that make gases unique from other forms of matter (solids and liquids). These include expandability, compressibility, and specific reactions to heat and pressure.

greenhouse gases The gases in Earth's atmosphere that let sunlight in but trap heat near the planet's surface.

matter Anything that occupies space.

methane hydrates Pieces of ice within which methane molecules are trapped.

molecule The smallest unit of a substance, generally one or more atoms joined tightly together.

natural gas A fossil fuel used for heating homes, composed mainly of methane.

physical changes The changes that can be observed but that don't alter the chemical composition of a substance.

pressure Any force that is applied to a surface.

volume The amount of space that matter takes up.

FOR MORE INFORMATION

American Chemical Society (ACS)
1155 Sixteenth Street NW
Washington, DC 20036
(800) 227-5558
Web site: http://www.acs.org
The ACS is a congressionally chartered organization that represents individuals in the field of chemistry. It prints educational books and periodicals pertaining to chemistry.

Carbon Footprint, Ltd.
Worthing House
Church Lane
Basingstoke, Hampshire RG23 8PX
England
Phone: 011-44-01256-345-645
Web site: http://www.carbonfootprint.com
Carbon Footprint is a carbon management consulting service that helps businesses reduce their carbon emissions. Its Web site has information on carbon emissions and a carbon footprint calculator.

National Research Council Canada (NRCC)
1200 Montreal Road, Building M-55
Ottawa, ON K1A 0R6
Canada

(613) 993-9084
Web site: http://www.nrc-cnrc.gc.ca
The NRCC is a scientific research organization run by the
    Canadian government since 1916. It publishes a monthly
    periodical called the *Canadian Journal of Chemistry*.

National Science Foundation (NSF)
4201 Wilson Boulevard
Arlington, VA 22230
(703) 292-5111
Web site: http://www.nsf.gov
The NSF is an independent federal agency created by
    Congress in 1950. Its Web site posts articles about recent
    scientific discoveries pertaining to gases.

Science Club
4921 Preston/Fall-City Road
Fall City, WA 98024
(425) 222-5066
Web site: http://scienceclub.org
The Science Club is a nonprofit organization dedicated to
    increasing curiosity about science through easy and fun
    experiments. All of the activities use common household
    materials and can be done at home.

YES Mag
501-3960 Quadra Street
Victoria, BC V8X 4A3
Canada

(888) 477-5543

Web site: http://www.yesmag.ca

YES Mag is a youth science magazine based in Canada. Its
Web site has frequently updated experiments that students
can try at home.

WEB SITES

Due to the changing nature of Internet links, Rosen Publishing
has developed an online list of Web sites related to the subject
of this book. This site is updated regularly. Please use this link
to access the list:

http://www.rosenlinks.com/sms/gatp

FOR FURTHER READING

Bily, Cynthia A. *Global Warming: Opposing Viewpoints*. New York, NY: Greenhaven Press, 2006.

Brown, Cynthia Light. *Amazing Kitchen Chemistry Projects You Can Build Yourself*. Chicago, IL: Nomad Press, 2008.

Clark, John O. E., and William Hemsley, eds. *Rosen Comprehensive Dictionary of Chemistry* (Rosen Comprehensive Student Dictionaries). New York, NY: Rosen Publishing Group, 2007.

Cobb, Cathy. *The Joy of Chemistry: The Amazing Science of Familiar Things*. Amherst, NY: Prometheus Books, 2005.

David, Sarah B. *Reducing Your Carbon Footprint at Home* (Your Carbon Footprint). New York, NY: Rosen Publishing Group, 2009.

Furgang, Adam. *The Noble Gases: Helium, Neon, Argon, Krypton, Xenon, Radon* (Understanding the Elements of the Periodic Table). New York, NY: Rosen Publishing Group, 2010.

Furgang, Kathy, and Adam Furgang. *On the Move: Green Transportation* (Your Carbon Footprint). New York, NY: Rosen Publishing Group, 2009.

Gonnick, Larry. *The Cartoon Guide to Chemistry*. New York, NY: Collins Reference, 2005.

McIntosh, Kenneth. *The Earth Cries Out: Forensic Chemistry and Environmental Science*. New York, NY: Mason Crest Publishers, 2008.

Morano-Kjelle, Marylou. *The Properties of Gases* (Library of Physical Science). New York, NY: PowerKids Press, 2007.

Nagle, Jeanne. *Reducing Your Carbon Footprint at School* (Your Carbon Footprint). New York, NY: Rosen Publishing Group, 2009.

Randolph, Joanne. *Gases in My World* (My World of Science). New York, NY: PowerKids Press, 2006.

Silverman, Buffy. *State of Confusion: Solids, Liquids, and Gases*. New York, NY: Raintree, 2007.

Sommers, Michael A. *Antarctic Melting: The Disappearing Antarctic Ice Cap* (Extreme Environmental Threats). New York, NY: Rosen Publishing Group, 2006.

West, Krista. *States of Matter: Gases, Liquids, and Solids*. New York, NY: Chelsea House, 2008.

Williams, Zella. *Experiments with Solids, Liquids, and Gases* (Do-It-Yourself Science). New York, NY: PowerKids Press, 2007.

BIBLIOGRAPHY

Brown, Cynthia Light. *Amazing Kitchen Chemistry Projects You Can Build Yourself*. Chicago, IL: Nomad Press, 2008.

Cobb, Cathy. *The Joy of Chemistry: The Amazing Science of Familiar Things*. Amherst, NY: Prometheus Books, 2005.

Gardner, Robert. *Experiments with Solids, Liquids, and Gases*. New York, NY: Enslow Publishers, 2000.

Halaszy, Gyorgy. *Carbon Capture and Greenhouse Gases*. Hauppauge, NY: Nova Science Publishers, 2010.

Houghton, John. *Global Warming: A Complete Briefing*. Cambridge, England: Cambridge University Press, 2009.

Kavanah, Patrick. *Chemistry: The Physical Setting*. Needham, MA: Pearson/Prentice Hall, 2009.

Loeb, Leonard B. *The Kinetic Theory of Gases*. Mineola, NY: Dover Publications, 2004.

Maynard, Barbara. "Are Methane Hydrates the World's Next Big Energy Source?" *Popular Mechanics*, April 2006. Retrieved February 2010 (http://www.popularmechanics.com/science/environment/2558946).

Merrill, Amy French. *Everyday Physical Science Experiments with Gases* (Science Surprises). New York, NY: PowerKids Press, 2002.

Poling, Bruce E., John M. Prausnitz, and John P. O'Connell. *The Properties of Gases and Liquids*. New York, NY: McGraw-Hill Professional, 2000.

Shachtman, Thomas. *Absolute Zero and the Conquest of Cold*. New York, NY: Mariner Books, 2000.

Sutton, Raul. *Chemistry for the Life Sciences*. Boca Raton, FL: CRC Press/Taylor & Francis Group, 2009.

Tocci, Salvatore. *Experiments with Solids, Liquids, and Gases*. New York, NY: Scholastic Press, 2001.

Wolfe, Joshua. *Climate Change: Picturing the Science*. New York, NY: W. W. Norton & Co., 2009.

Zhou, Yue, et al. "Experimental Investigation of Methane Gas Production from Methane Hydrate." *Industrial & Engineering Chemistry Research*, 2009; 48 (6): 3,142–3,149.

INDEX

ABOUT THE AUTHOR

Susan Meyer is a writer and science enthusiast. Meyer lives in Queens, New York, where she does her part to reduce greenhouse gas emissions and combat global warming by not owning a car.

PHOTO CREDITS

Designer: Sam Zavieh; Photo Researcher: Marty Levick